TALES
OF OLD CINCINNATI

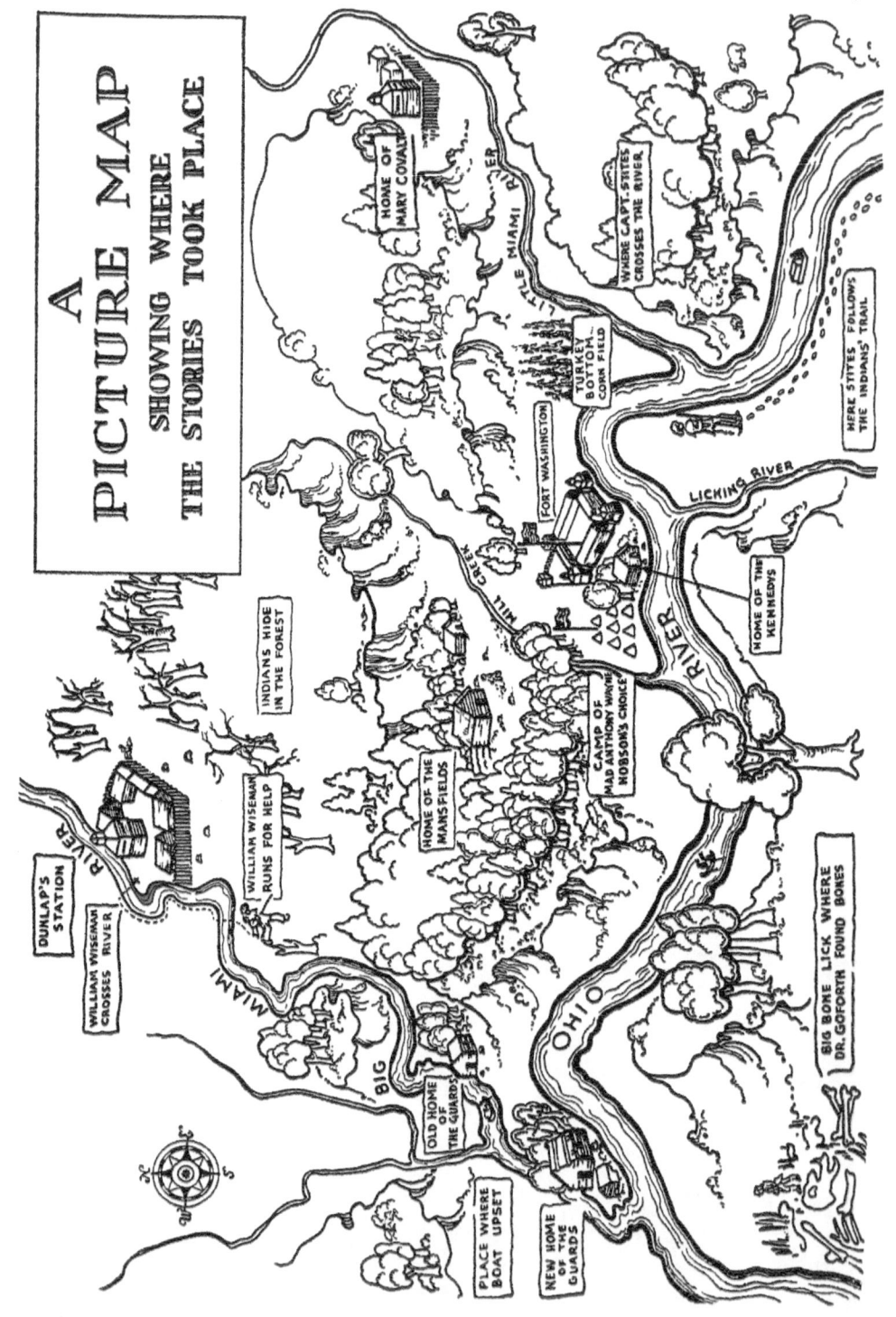

TALES OF OLD CINCINNATI

COMPILED BY
WORKERS OF THE WRITERS' PROGRAM
WORKS PROGRESS ADMINISTRATION IN THE STATE OF OHIO
1940

COMMONWEALTH BOOK COMPANY
ST. MARTIN, OHIO
2024

Copyright © 1940 by The Hamilton County Good Government League
This edition copyright © 2024 by Commonwealth Book Company, Inc.

All rights reserved. No part of this book may be reproduced in any form or by any means without the prior written consent of the publisher, excepting brief quotes used in reviews. Printed in the United States of America.

ISBN: 978-1-948986-77-9

• Preface

TALES OF OLD CINCINNATI is a book of stories about the Cincinnati frontier. They tell of exploration and high adventure, of settlement and home life. Mainly, they are stories about people. They have much to say about how the pioneers came, how they worked and played, and what they did about their troubles. These tales are enlivened a little by fancy, but basically they are true. The people in them were once alive, and they did what you read in this book.

The first draft of these stories was written by the Federal Writers' Project, directed by Dr. Harlan H. Hatcher; the final manuscript was done by the Ohio Writers' Project and checked in the district supervised by Robert M. Ross. For the illustrations we are indebted to the Cleveland unit of the Ohio Art Project (Kalman Kubinyi, District Supervisor), directed by Charlotte Gowing Cooper. We have tried to adapt the book to the use and enjoyment of grade school children.

We thank the officials of the Cincinnati Public Schools and of the Hamilton County Good Government League (particularly Judge John C. Dempsey) who helped us with suggestions and encouragement.

HARRY GRAFF, State Supervisor
• The Ohio Writers' Project

• They Use Fire

Towards sundown, Simon Girty called again. He sent Abner Hunt, who was still tied, near enough to speak to the settlers.

"The Indians are going away to eat supper now," Hunt said. "When the moon goes down, they will return. They say they are determined to slay all of you and torture me to death."

The Indians then took Hunt and went a little way into the woods. They left a few warriors to watch the fort.

As they waited for the Indians to come back, the men in the station looked at their bullets. They had only a few left. They wondered what they would do when these would be used up.

The women and girls in the cabins got busy. They lit hickory and maple wood in the fireplaces. Then they melted in a ladle over the hot fire all their pewter plates and cups and spoons and everything else that would melt. When the pewter was melted, they poured it into molds and made bullets. The work was hot and slow and hard, but after a while the women had a few bullets they could give to the men. These would help keep the Indians away a while longer.

As darkness came the rain stopped and the skies cleared. A dim and misty moon shone over the little station and on the dead Indians who lay just outside the walls. The white men waited. Every few minutes they looked up at the moon.

Soon they could not see the moon, and the rain poured down again. Then shots and yells came from the forest, and the settlers knew that the Indians had come back rested and fed.

The men in the station listened calmly to the wild war cries. Their hands were numb, their clothing was stiff with ice, and they were hungry. But they stood at their places. They were even more cautious than they had been during the day, because the Indians might be crawling up to the stockade wall.

One soldier suddenly whispered to another a few feet away, "What's that fire over there?"

The other looked, and saw a tiny tongue of flame flickering through the dark. Soon it grew, and many more began to come up all around the fort.

"They're going to try to burn us out," Lieutenant Kingsbury said.

By the light of the fires the white men saw the Indians break short branches off the fallen trees about the fort. They held one end of each branch in a fire until the wood was flaming.

"Look out! Here comes one," a soldier cried, as an Indian put a flaming stick to his bow and sent it over the fort walls. It looked like a falling star. It came hissing and sputtering inside the fort. As a woman ran from one of the cabins to put it out, dozens of other fire sticks fell on the roofs of the cabins, by the log walls, and against the fort.

They Demand Surrender •

The Indians were disappointed. They had planned to sneak up on the fort at daylight, climb over the walls, and surprise the settlers in their beds. When they were met by gunfire, they knew their first plan would not work. So they hid themselves behind trees and piles of logs.

The leader of the Indians was a white man named Simon Girty. He lay behind a log and called to Lieutenant Kingsbury. He asked the Lieutenant to order his soldiers to stop firing. Girty said he wished to talk with the Lieutenant.

Lieutenant Kingsbury told his men to take their fingers from their triggers. When the place was quiet, everyone in the station crowded forward to the stockade to see what was going to happen. There, a few feet from Simon Girty, stood a man. His wrists were tied with leather cords. One end of a rope was fastened to his waist. The other end was held by Simon Girty, so that the man could not run away.

This prisoner standing near the stockade was Abner Hunt, the surveyor whom the Indians had taken prisoner three days before. He looked at his white friends in the station and they looked at him as Simon Girty talked to Lieutenant Kingsbury.

"There are 500 Indians here," Girty said. "Scattered through the woods are 300 more. They are led by me and by a famous chief—Blue Jacket! If you do not surrender, we shall torture Abner Hunt to death and kill all of you. We shall slay any man who tries to escape to Fort Washington. If he does get away from the fort alive, my scouts will catch and kill him in the woods."

Lieutenant Kingsbury stood on a stump inside the stockade and listened. When Girty had finished, the Lieutenant shook his fist at him and shouted, "We shall never surrender."

He leaped from the stump to the ground as bullets from the guns of the Indians whizzed over the stockade. The men within the stockade fired back. The air was so filled with smoke that no one could see. When the smoke cleared away, there on the ground lay the white plume of Lieutenant Kingsbury's hat. Kingsbury himself was unharmed.

As the day continued slowly, the Indians kept firing. A heavy rain fell. Then it grew so cold that a thin layer of ice lay on the ground and on the men's clothes.

But the men did not go into the cabins to warm themselves, nor did they walk around to take the numbness from their feet and hands. They stood perfectly still, with their eyes hunting out the Indians. When an Indian showed himself, a settler fired at him.

The only food the men had was parched corn, which was brought them by the girls of the station—Sarah and Salome Hahn and Rebecca Grum. The only drink they had was rain water, for the Indians would have shot anyone who tried to get a bucket of water from the river.

• The Indians Gather

For several days the Indians did not come near the station. Then, on a Saturday evening, the fifth of February, the people of the station suddenly heard a knocking and calling at the heavy gate. Several soldiers ran to open it. They found a man out of breath and covered with blood from a bad wound.

Lieutenant Kingsbury took the man to his room in the fort. There the man told his story. His name was Sloan. Together with Abner Hunt and another man, he had been surveying in the woods. A party of Indians had attacked them, taken Abner Hunt prisoner, and killed the other man. They had wounded Mr. Sloan. In spite of his wounds, he had run away and reached Dunlap's Station.

Lieutenant Kingsbury gave Mr. Sloan his own room and bed. He himself went to stay with his men.

The next morning, the Lieutenant sent five soldiers to look for the body of the man the Indians had killed. The soldiers found the dead man, buried him, and returned safely to the fort. When they said they had seen no sign of Indians, the settlers were glad. Maybe the Indians had all gone away and would do no more harm.

Sunday passed quietly. Mr. Sloan began to look better. But Lieutenant Kingsbury let him sleep, and himself spent Sunday night with the soldiers.

The Lieutenant did not sleep so well. In the early morning he heard a dog bark wildly. He sprang up and rushed outside. A great black dog was growling on top of one of the log cabins.

Lieutenant Kingsbury knew that something had scared the dog. He ran to the log walls and looked into the forest. The morning light was dim and blue, but not too faint to see by. He put his hands to his mouth and yelled as loud as he could, "Indians! Indians!"

The woods, the fort, and the cabins shook with noise and confusion. Women screamed, babies cried, dogs barked. Soldiers sprang from their beds, grabbed their guns, and jumped, half-dressed, to the stockade.

The Indians crept in the woods and surrounded the stockade. They were tall and fierce and wild. They shouted their war cries, and waved and fired their guns. Their faces were smeared with red and white clay, and long feathers were stuck in their hair.

Lieutenant Kingsbury wasted no time looking at the enemy. He had only the 13 soldiers he had brought and the 10 men and boys of the fort. He knew, and the men and boys knew, that each of them would die rather than let the Indians take Dunlap's Station.

The Lieutenant placed the men and boys at windows and loopholes in the cabins and also at places along the wall. To each of them he said, "Stand here until I tell you to move."

5
Siege at Dunlap's

• The Lieutenant Gets A Recruit

IT was a cold winter day late in January. General Harmar stood beside the fire in his cabin at Fort Washington. He kicked a few burning logs over, so that they would flame up faster. Then he walked back and forth in the room.

General Harmar was not only cold. He was also worried. He had just received word that the settlers at a place called Dunlap's Station were about to be attacked by the Indians. He walked and thought a long time. Then he sent for Lieutenant Kingsbury.

When the Lieutenant came, General Harmar told him what was in his mind.

"We have only a few soldiers here," he said. "They are hardly enough to guard Cincinnati and Columbia. Yet we must help these people 17 miles away. So I want you to take about a dozen soldiers and ride fast to Dunlap's Station before the Indians get there to destroy its people."

Lieutenant Kingsbury saluted and left. He chose 12 of the best soldiers in the fort. Then the Lieutenant noticed a young recruit looking as if he wanted to go along.

"You, there," cried the Lieutenant, "what's your name?"

"William Wiseman," the boy replied.

"Get on a horse and come along," shouted Lieutenant Kingsbury.

William's eyes were glad as he ran towards his horse, jumped into the saddle, and rode back to the Lieutenant. The other men had also mounted horses. They all rode through the gate of the stockade into the village streets of Cincinnati. People stopped their work and watched the soldiers as they jogged past. The soldiers had to go slow because hogs and cows stood with their noses low in the streets.

The Lieutenant and his men rode westward to shallow Mill Creek. Then they took a trail through the bare sycamores along the stream, and let the wind spank their faces as they hurried toward Dunlap's Station.

After about two hours, the Lieutenant and his men trotted from the cold forest up to the Great Miami River. There beside it was Dunlap's Station, a place of several cabins within a stockade.

After his men had rested and eaten, Lieutenant Kingsbury ordered them to cut down the trees growing near three sides of the stockade.

"We don't have to worry about being attacked from the river side," he said, "but the Indians could slip upon us from behind all these trees."

• "Indians! Indians!"

Indians Change Their Plans •

One morning Captain Covalt, two of his sons, and Joseph Hinkle, another settler of the station, were hard at work. Suddenly a party of Indians sprang from the bushes. The settlers had no chance to get their guns. The men and boys started to run. One Indian killed Mr. Hinkle with his tomahawk. Two Indians fired at Captain Covalt and wounded him.

"Run home as fast as you can," Captain Covalt cried to his sons.

The boys reached the station safely. But when Captain Covalt had gone about a hundred yards, he became too weak to go farther. He fell across a log. The Indians sprang on Captain Covalt and scalped him.

Mrs. Covalt, Mary, and the other children mourned Captain Covalt's death. Then they wondered whether they should finish their house and live in it. They decided not to move outside the station. Mrs. Covalt said, "Some day a great general will gather an army and march against the Indians. When the Indians are driven away, we'll go out upon our land. Then we'll finish building our home, and live together as happily as we can, remembering your father and your brother Abraham."

One day word came that General St. Clair was forming a great army. Mary's older brother and many other young men of the station went away to Cincinnati to join General St. Clair's army. The women and children waited at home for their men. They waited a long time. Of all the men from Covalt's Station who went to fight with General St. Clair, only one came back. He was one of Mary's brothers.

A neighbor said to Mrs. Covalt, "You have only one son left to protect you. Why don't you return with us to Pennsylvania? There you and the few children you have left will be safe."

Mrs. Covalt shook her head. "I have lost Mr. Covalt and all my boys but one. Yet we are all here together. We love the Ohio wilderness. We shall stay."

Mrs. Covalt lived until she was 104 years old. She lived to see her grandchildren play safely in the woods and help their fathers plant corn without having to be afraid of Indians.

And what happened to Mary? She grew into a fine young lady and married a man named Joseph Jones. Yes, she was the Mrs. Jones who wrote down all these things about Covalt's Station.

• The Covalts Work And Plan

When the cabins were completed, Captain Covalt and his men, and also the boys, started to get the ground ready for planting corn and potatoes. They cut down trees and cleared away the underbrush and weeds.

Captain Covalt had a little girl named Mary, who was about 15 years old. Mary was busy at home with her mother. There was much work for a girl to do. Wool from the sheep had to be spun into yarn, which was woven into cloth. The cloth was sewed by hand into clothing. Besides working with the wool, Mary had to cook and mend and clean.

Soap for cleaning had to be made from scraps of fat and lye. The making of the lye was not an easy job. All the ashes from the wood burned in the fireplace were saved and put into a large hopper. Water was poured over the ashes to get out the lye. This water was then boiled down and cooked with the fat to make soap.

The women and girls of Covalt Station also used the lye water for other things. Sometimes whole grains of corn were boiled in it until the covering of the corn grew soft and fell away. The corn was then washed many times in clean water. Next it was cooked until the grain was large and soft. This they called hominy. They liked to eat hominy along with the meat from the game the men killed in the forest.

In the evening and in the morning Mary helped milk the cows. One night, as she walked into the stable, she saw an Indian's eyes peeking at her through a crack in the wall. Mary called for her father. The Indian ran away.

As the months passed, the Indians grew bolder. They stole five of Captain Covalt's fine horses and some of his sheep and hogs. They watched the station all the time from the woods. It was risky to go through the woods. Mary's brother Abraham, who was 21 years old, was killed while hunting. Abel Cook, his friend, was slain while making a trip to Columbia.

Mary and her mother heard about this, and feared for the safety of Captain Covalt and the boys. Mornings, when Captain Covalt went away to work in the fields, or the boys entered the forest to hunt, the women and girls watched them go. As they waved goodbye to the men and boys, they wondered whether all would come back alive in the evening. But neither the women nor the girls complained or cried. That would not help any.

Captain Covalt had bought 600 acres of land near the station. In spite of the danger, he now wanted to move onto this land. He planned to build a home in a clearing he had made in the woods. Each day he and his older boys would take their guns and go to this clearing. Soon logs for walls were ready to be lifted into place. Only the split roofing-boards and door and window frames had yet to be made.

4
Mary Covalt

• Mrs. Jones Tells A Story

ALL the people who came to settle the Ohio Country did not stop at Columbia or Cincinnati. Some went up the two Miami Rivers or back into the hills. They did not live apart, as farmers do now. Instead, they stayed together for protection against the Indians. They put all their cabins on a small plot of ground, and around them built strong log walls with blockhouses at each corner. The walls were called a stockade. The whole community was known as a station.

The people of Cincinnati and Columbia were so close to Fort Washington, which had many soldiers, that the Indians seldom tried to attack them. But the stations in the hills had only a few men and boys to protect them. So the Indians bothered those stations. They would often dash from the thick woods, yelling and firing at the settlers. They also stole horses and cows left to graze in the woods. Sometimes they killed or captured men hunting game for their families, and boys who wandered into the woods for grapes or chestnuts or hickory nuts.

When the men went out of the stockade to clear the ground of trees or plant their corn, they always carried rifles. The men who hoed kept their guns leaning on a log or stump within easy reach.

The women and children stayed behind the stockade walls. But even they were always watching for Indians. When the men were away, the women and older girls kept guns beside them, for sometimes an Indian's head would come peering over the stockade.

In later days, when the country was free of Indians, the wives and daughters of the first settlers told stories of those dangerous early times. A woman named Mrs. Joseph Jones knew more tales than anyone else. She wrote down some of her stories. By reading them we know something of the troubles and hardships at Covalt's Station, where she lived when she was a little girl.

Covalt's Station was named for Captain Covalt. On New Year's Day in 1789, Captain Covalt, Mrs. Covalt, and their 10 children left Pennsylvania in two flatboats. The boats were crowded with furniture and farm tools, 20 head of cattle, seven of the finest horses that had yet come to Ohio, and several sheep and hogs.

In spite of cold weather and chunks of floating ice in the river, they came at last to the Little Miami River, near Columbia. Captain Covalt and his party traveled up the Little Miami to a place called Round Bottom, about two miles below what is now Milford. There the men began to build cabins.

• They waved goodbye

It Makes Food For Winter •

Soon the ears stood up above the blades. They were plump and heavy in their thick layers of green husks. The plant no longer needed the silks at the end of each ear, and they grew brown and dried. The men walked among the corn rows, and looked up at the giant stalks. Some of the tassels were more than 14 feet above the ground. The men tore open a little of the husk of an ear, and looked inside. When they pressed their thumb into a kernel, the kernel popped open and showed white.

"Now the corn is good for roasting," the men said.

They filled their arms with the green corn, but left most of it standing in the field.

The women boiled some of the corn on the cob. Some they cut from the cob and fried, or cooked with green beans, and called the stuff succotash. No matter how it was fixed, the corn tasted good.

As summer turned into autumn, the grain of the corn grew harder and the tops of the husks were brown. The women took the hard corn and ground it into meal for corn bread.

Meanwhile, the men gathered the beans and cut the cornstalks, which they tied together into fat bundles, or shocks. The yellow-brown stalks and blades of the corn they called fodder. Through the winter the cows and horses would eat the fodder.

The people had plenty of bread that year. When the men went far to hunt, they carried leather bags of parched corn and hominy. The women sometimes stuffed the husks of the corn into ticks, or slips, and thus had mattresses.

And as their parents and the older brothers and sisters sat shelling the corn, the small children played before the log fire and built houses of red and yellow cobs. They were not afraid of the wolves and the cold. They were strong and happy. They remembered that their wise mothers had said a friend would bring bread. They had been expecting a man to come carrying armsful of bread. They now knew that their strong friend was the corn plant, which gave food to the hungry.

• Summer Brings Corn

The boys and girls did not spend all their time gathering wildflowers or calling to the birds and animals. Sometimes they went to Turkey Bottom to see the men and larger boys get ready to plant corn.

After the fields were plowed, the men made shallow holes, about four feet apart. In each of these holes the children put five grains. As they dropped the seeds, they sometimes sang:

> One for the squirrel,
> And one for the crow.
> Three to sprout,
> And two to grow.

The men then took hoes and spread earth over the holes.

They waited eagerly for the seeds to push up their little green heads. After a time they saw green things like grass peeping from the soil. They knew that the seeds were sprouting.

"We must not let the crows, squirrels, and chipmunks dig it up for the grain at its roots," the men told the children.

When corn comes up from the ground, it is a weak little plant with not enough roots to take its food from the soil. Instead, it feeds on the grain from which it sprouted, until its roots are strong enough to help themselves.

The crows knew about the grain at the root of each plant. They circled over the field and screamed, "Caw, caw." They flew down and jerked up young plants. Sometimes the squirrels and chipmunks would sneak over and work down to the grain with their front paws.

Soon the corn grew stronger. It was as high as the children's knees. The men hoed the corn again. When it was waist-high, they hoed it a last time. Now there was nothing to do but watch it grow.

One day green fibers showed between the top blades of many corn plants. "The corn is in tassel now," the men said. They smiled to see the corn had grown so tall the tassels dangled high above them.

Just below the tassel, one or two ears of corn soon peeped between the broad green blades and the stalk. Each ear was tipped with a bundle of long, green threads of corn silk. Each thread was a hollow tube leading to a small, pale blister hidden under the green wrappings of the young ear.

When the wind blew, the great stalks bowed and whispered, and high overhead the tassels shook out pollen like gold dust. Sometimes it fell upon the children or upon small animals as they romped among the corn rows. If the children or the animals or the wind brushed against one of the silks at the end of the young ears of corn, a grain of pollen sometimes fell into the hollow silk. It then traveled to the blister on the ear of corn. When the bit of pollen had reached the ear, the grain of corn at the bottom of the silk began to grow.

3
The Strong Friend

• Hungry Pioneers Welcome Spring

THE first winter for the Columbia settlers was long and cold. It snowed hard. The children shivered in their beds as they heard wolves howling in the hills through the dark winter nights.

The heavy snow and the noise of the wolves were not the worst things about the winter. Food was scarce. The nearest stores were a hundred miles up the Ohio River. Because of the ice in the river, food could not be brought on the flatboats. There were times when the children were so hungry they almost cried. Their fathers killed game for meat in the forest, but there was no bread to eat with it.

The Indians gave them some corn, but not enough to make bread for everybody. The pioneer women dug roots from under the snow, and pounded them into a kind of bread. But it was not good bread. Nor did it keep the children from getting hungry.

All through the winter, Captain Stites and the other men would say, "Winter will go away soon. Watch those dogwood and redbud trees on the hills and the sycamores on the river bank. When their leaves come out, there will be happy animals and birds in the woods. You'll be able to go out and play, and you'll feel much better."

The women smiled, and said to the children, "You mustn't be afraid of the noisy wolves, or cry because you are cold and haven't good bread. Soon a friend will bring us food."

The children listened and wondered who this friend could be. At night they dreamed of sunny days and of a stranger carrying many loaves of bread.

March came with quick, wild winds, and April brought warm rains. May was soft and mellow. In the hills the dogwood and redbud trees became starry with flowers. Beside the Ohio the little sycamore leaves were pale green and tender. The children found wild poppies and lady's slippers on the river hill. The women put on their bonnets and went hunting wild greens in Turkey Bottom.

In the woods, birds were happy as they made their nests. The children were surprised that there were so many and that they were so beautiful. They saw redbirds, blue jays, finches, thrushes, and woodpeckers. They liked especially to watch the bright-colored parakeets. Today children can see parakeets like these only in the museum.

There were many animals, too. The Stites children and their playmates stood many hours looking at squirrels playing among the trees. If they saw a fox or a bear, they ran home as fast as they could.

• One for the squirrel

It Stands In The Wrong Place •

Next the men built a door of wide, thick planks. The door hung on pegs, for there were no hinges. Then the windows had to be made. Instead of being wide panes of clear glass such as we have today, they were only small squares of greased paper. The paper let in a bit of light, but could not be seen through.

The huge fireplace at one side of the room gave heat and light on winter evenings. It also helped make the tasty meals of the settlers. Bread was baked in the heavy iron Dutch ovens buried in the coals. Meat was broiled in skillets set on the fire. Water was boiled in the kettles that hung on cranes or poles of green wood above the flames.

The other three log cabins in Losantiville had only hard clay for floors, but Mr. Kennedy wanted something better for his family. He took some of the boat planks in the camp and used them for the floor of his house.

Sometimes the Kennedys wondered a little where they lived. There were so many trees around, that perhaps their address was not the corner of Walnut and Front Streets. When spring came and the trees were heavy with leaves, Mr. Ludlow and the surveyors cleared more ground and made streets through the forest.

Then one day the whole family and all the other people of Losantiville had a great surprise. The Kennedy home was not at the corner of two streets as they had supposed. It was right in the middle of Water Street.

Mr. Kennedy and Colonel Ludlow and all the other men laughed and laughed. But Rebecca stood and cried.

"Daddy," she sobbed, "now we'll have to take our nice new home apart."

Mr. Kennedy looked at Mr. Ludlow. The Colonel smiled, and pulled Rebecca into his arms.

"No, my child," he said. "Strong, honest work never goes to waste. Anyway, other townsmen have planted their potato patches in the street, so why shouldn't your father put up his log cabin there? I would rather not have the street cut through at all than tear down the beautiful new home of the best-behaved little girl in Losantiville."

• Mr. Kennedy Builds A House

For the next few days, while Mrs. Kennedy kept house in the flatboat, Mr. Kennedy worked in Losantiville. He helped Colonel Ludlow and the other men cut down trees and lay out streets. Sometimes he went with them to hunt for bear or deer or wild turkeys.

When the weather was fair and not too cold, the older Kennedy children left their boat and romped on the river bank. They played "Follow the Leader" along the river and around the trunks of the great trees. And sometimes, when they wanted to sing and were a little tired, they would gather around and play "Farmer in the Dell" and "London Bridge is Falling Down."

There were many days when they could not leave their boat because of the heavy snow and ice. As spring neared and the ice began to melt, frozen chunks were loosened and sent swiftly down the river. One day several pieces of ice passed dangerously near the Kennedy boat.

"We'll have to move," Mr. Kennedy said.

There was not time to build a log cabin. So the men took apart the boat and built a camp for the family to live in till Mr. Kennedy could make a real home. The Kennedys lived in the camp for six weeks.

Meanwhile Mr. Kennedy began to build a new home at the corner of what he supposed was Walnut and Front Streets.

There was much work to do. Mr. Kennedy chopped down the sycamores, oaks, maples, and other trees that grew where his house and yard were to be. He rolled some of the trunks out of the way, but saved the best ones. He took the bark and branches off them with an ax, and hewed them down until they were flat on two sides. With these he would make the walls of his house. He split some logs into thick, rough boards. These he called clapboards. They would be for the roof of the home. He planned to use other logs for door and window frames.

Rebecca thought to herself that her father's house would be the finest in the settlement. She wished she were a boy, so that she could use a knife. She might then make the stout oak pegs with which her father hung the doors and fastened boards for the roof.

At last logs for the walls were ready to be lifted into place. The logs were long, thick, and heavy. One man alone could never have picked them up. So all the men of Losantiville came to help Mr. Kennedy.

Although Mr. Kennedy fitted the logs together carefully, there were cracks in the walls. He put mud in these holes. Next, he built a chimney by fitting sticks together. He plastered the inside of the chimney with plenty of clay to keep the sticks from catching fire.

The men put small timbers above the walls for the frame of the roof. Over this frame they laid the clapboards. They weighted the clapboards down with poles so they would not blow away in the wind or slide off the sloping roof. The poles were fastened with pegs and braces.

2
The New Home

• The Kennedys Reach Losantiville

REBECCA Kennedy waited with her father and mother and six brothers and sisters as her family's flatboat rounded a bend in the Ohio River. She stood on tiptoe as she looked eagerly for Losantiville, the place that was to be her new home.

"I can't see anything but hills and trees," one of her younger brothers complained.

"We're not there yet. We passed Columbia only a little while ago," Mrs. Kennedy said, as she shifted her baby from one arm to the other.

"Don't worry, it won't run away from us," the father added. He stood near the front of the boat and guided it with a pole through the swift, muddy water. He, as well as his wife and children, would be glad to see other people and to walk about a bit on land. They had been on the flatboat for days, with little to do but watch the swift water or look at the tall trees along the river bank. Now it was early February. Cold rains and snow had formed pieces of ice in the Ohio, and the boat was always in danger of being crushed by the thick ice.

The river carried the family around another bend, and Rebecca suddenly found herself jumping up and down, crying, "We're here. I see a log cabin."

"There are three of them," one of her brothers exclaimed.

It took Mr. Kennedy only a little while to get the boat to shore. It had scarcely touched land, when all the children went rushing up the river bank. They were so eager to be in the town that they did not see the two gentlemen who came down the hill to greet the Kennedy family. The men hurried up to Mr. and Mrs. Kennedy and shook hands. "Welcome to Losantiville," they said, and introduced themselves as Israel Ludlow and William McMillan.

They walked about and showed the Kennedys what had been done. There were three small log cabins, with floors of hard-packed clay and chimneys of sticks and mud. Great logs and many wide stumps were near the cabins. And around them rose a forest of trees taller and thicker than those we see nowadays.

Colonel Ludlow and other men thought that some day the three cabins would grow into a town. They had planned streets through the trees and had marked off places for houses. Notches on the tree trunks showed where streets would run. But there were so many trees that it was hard to tell where the streets began and where they ended.

• They played "Follow the Leader"

He Comes Back Without Horses •

Captain Stites thought a long while and smiled to himself. Then he spoke to his men: "I guess you were right. We wouldn't have a chance against all those Indians. Besides, we have something better to do than look for horses."

The men wondered at what he said, but they were glad to start home. They thought that Captain Stites would lead them back the way they had come. They did not know that he was not really afraid of the Indians. He simply wanted to see more of the fine new country.

The men agreed to go with him west across the hills. They entered the wide, fertile valley of the Great Miami River, followed the stream, then turned left over the hills, and at last reached Mill Creek. They picked their way along Mill Creek to the Ohio River and returned to Washington, Kentucky.

All the people who had remained in the town welcomed the men heartily. They looked around for the horses they thought the party had rescued from the Indians. They saw none. The people were surprised, and they all went up to Captain Stites.

"Where are our horses?" they demanded.

Captain Stites pretended to be puzzled at their question.

"What horses?" he asked.

"The ones the Indians took and you went after," they replied impatiently. They wondered whether Captain Stites had lost his mind in the deep forests.

Captain Stites knew what they were thinking, and his eyes twinkled.

"Oh yes, the horses. Well, you see, we couldn't get them, because there were too many Indians."

The people made long faces. They were disappointed.

"Then your trip was for nothing," they said.

"My friends," the Captain answered, "I did not get your horses, but I have found something far better than horses—a rich land of danger and beauty where I shall soon found a new settlement."

After speaking these fine words, Captain Stites went to pack up his things and say goodbye to his friends. Then he made the long trip to New York. There he arranged to buy 20,000 acres of land along the Ohio River beside the Little Miami River. In the fall of 1788, two years after he had looked for horses, Captain Stites and 26 other people came down the Ohio. They landed near the Little Miami River and built a town called Columbia, which is now part of Cincinnati.

• He Goes After Horses

Stites was confident. "I am a soldier," he said, "and I'm sure we can take care of the Indians we meet."

At last a group of men agreed to go.

The tracks of horses were fresh in the ground, making the trail easy to follow. It led back to the Ohio River and along the shore for almost forty miles to a place opposite the mouth of a stream. The men then saw that the Indians had made a raft and crossed the Ohio with the stolen horses.

Stites and the other men had heard of this neighborhood. A few miles down the Ohio near the mouth of the Licking River was the path the Indians usually followed when they came from their towns on the Great Lakes to get game and to plunder in Kentucky. On the land between the Great Miami and the Little Miami Rivers the Indians had fought battles among themselves, and they had also killed stray white men passing by. This place was to become known as the "Miami Slaughterhouse."

None of the men had ever gone into the deep forests that stretched away north. They knew that Indian towns lay hidden in the northern forests. They thought of their comfortable cabins and of their families, but their leader was determined to go on. "Let's follow them," he said.

The white men built a raft, slid it into the water, and got aboard. By pushing long poles against the bottom of the river, the men sent the raft to the opposite shore. The trail led up the valley of the Little Miami.

As Stites and his men followed the trail beside the little river, they saw why the Indians prized their lands. On the hillsides stood huge oak, beech, sugar maple, yellow poplar, hickory, and chestnut trees, many with trunks thicker than a man is tall. The men went by bluffs showing layers of stone, and they sometimes stepped into pure, soft clay. The soil in the broad valley was rich and loose. Sometimes the men saw deer, bear, and wild turkeys among the trees or at the many clear springs and creeks.

Captain Stites knew the value of all these things. The trees would make excellent logs for houses and for firewood, and the clay and stone could be used later to build larger homes. The nuts, such as the acorn off the oak, could make hogs fat and tasty. Fine crops of wheat and corn and potatoes could be grown in the mellow soil, and the forest animals would supply whatever else was necessary to feed hearty frontier folk. Here was a splendid place to live in!

Captain Stites looked around him and marveled as he followed the trail of the stolen horses farther up the river, deeper into the great forests. The men came to the headwaters of the Little Miami, and knew that they were close to an Indian town. Many Indians would be there, and they would not be friendly.

1
Better Than Horses

• A Trader Hears Of Robbery

IT was spring of the year 1786, and the Ohio River was broad and full. The flatboat carrying Captain Benjamin Stites, of Redstone, Pennsylvania, turned a big bend. There on the Kentucky shore, almost hidden among the many trees, were the log houses of 15 families. The little settlement was called Limestone.

Captain Stites had been on his flatboat almost a week, and the journey down the Ohio had been lonesome and dangerous. On the way he had seen few people except some Indians staring at his boat from the river bank. Captain Stites had not been afraid of them. His boat was big and strong, and it was covered at one end by bullet-proof timbers. Besides, the Captain himself was a tall, husky man who knew how to use his long rifle.

The river itself had given him the most serious trouble. Several times, logs sliding past in the current had almost smashed the boat. Branches caught in shallow parts of the river had rammed it. And Captain Stites had watched carefully for sand bars which might have grounded the flatboat.

Captain Stites was therefore glad when his boat drew even with Limestone. He took up a long pole and pushed it into the river bottom. The boat was thus guided to shore. As Stites tied it to a tree on the river bank, most of the people in Limestone hurried to learn whether they were about to welcome a new neighbor or a merchant. Captain Stites and the people of Limestone were disappointed. He had not come to live in Limestone, and they did not need the flour and meal and other things he had brought to sell. Stites, however, learned that a few miles back from the river there was a small settlement called Washington. He packed his goods and went there to sell them.

One morning, after Stites had been in Washington a few days and disposed of some supplies, he heard angry, excited talk. He soon learned that the Indians had stolen a number of horses from the settlers. It had happened before, this stealing by Indians who came down from the northern forests and crossed the Ohio River into Kentucky. The men feared that the Indians would keep on stealing until they had taken all the farm animals.

"Let's go after them and get the horses," said Captain Stites.

The men of Washington hesitated, for there might be many Indians.

• To the opposite shore

Contents •

1. BETTER THAN HORSES • A trader hears of robbery; he goes after horses; he comes back without horses. . . . . Page five

2. THE NEW HOME • The Kennedys reach Losantiville; Mr. Kennedy builds a house; it stands in the wrong place. . . . . Page nine

3. THE STRONG FRIEND • Hungry pioneers welcome spring; summer brings corn; it makes food for winter. . . . . Page thirteen

4. MARY COVALT • Mrs. Jones tells a story; the Covalts work and plan; Indians change their plans. . . . . Page seventeen

5. SIEGE AT DUNLAP'S • The Lieutenant gets a recruit; the Indians gather; they demand surrender; they use fire; the recruit makes good. . . Page twenty-one

6. THE LONG WALK • William runs to the river; he almost drowns; he brings help. . Page twenty-seven

7. MOTHER FINDS A WAY • The river upsets a boat; Mrs. Guard has a problem; she solves it. Page thirty-one

8. BIG WIND • Bad news comes from the north; good news comes from the east; big wind sweeps through the north. . . . . Page thirty-five

9. DOCTOR GOFORTH AND THE COLLAPSIBLE LION • The Doctor is a dandy; old bones lead him astray; he brings them back; they go abroad; they do strange things. . . . . Page thirty-nine

10. THE PLAYMATES • Edward gets a gift; it changes into ducks; the ducks make mischief; they take a trip. . . . . Page forty-five

ILLUSTRATED BY •
Gladys Carambella,
The Ohio Art Project

The Recruit Makes Good •

While the men kept back the Indians with their bullets, the women and girls fought the fires. They beat the big fires out with blankets, and smothered the small ones with their hands. The sleety rain helped, too, so that the fort did not catch on fire.

The sticks continued to come flaming and hissing over the walls until midnight. Then most of the Indians went away in the woods.

The settlers and the soldiers listened and waited. Their faces were pale and their eyes looked worried. They knew what the Indians were going to do. Soon they heard the screams of Abner Hunt as the Indians tortured him. At dawn the forest was still.

When daylight came, the Indians again drew close to the fort. They had been happy all night. They were sure they would win.

The women and children had gathered in the blockhouse, which was the largest building in the little station. They were brave, but tired and almost without hope. When Lieutenant Kingsbury came into the room to stand a moment by the fire, they all came up and begged him to think of some way to save them.

"We must all suffer and die together," he said, and looked into the low fire. "I don't know of a way out. We can't get anyone to help us, and we can't hold out much longer. I have written a letter to General Harmar at Fort Washington, telling him we need more men. But none of our men dares to take the message to the General. Everyone knows there is little chance of getting past Simon Girty and his Indians."

Near a loophole on the other side of the blockhouse stood William Wiseman. About an hour ago he had come from his post by the outside wall to this loophole in the blockhouse. His clothing was wet and his feet were numb, but he had not taken time to warm himself by the fire.

He heard the terror in the women's voices and the misery in the children's crying. He heard what Lieutenant Kingsbury said.

"You've not asked *me*, sir," he said to Lieutenant Kingsbury, without turning his head.

The Lieutenant slapped him on the shoulder. "I never thought of you, when men older and stronger than you wouldn't go. I'll give you two half-joes if you'll try."

Two half-joes were two pieces of gold worth eight dollars. Each soldier's pay was three dollars a month, so that eight dollars was a good reward for the task.

The young soldier shook his head, "I am not doing this for money. I only want the other men to stand and watch me. They will see that we can beat the Indians with the courage we have shown so far. I will take the letter to General Harmar."

With these brave words, William got ready to leave.

What happened to him is told in the next story.

• He walked into the water

6
The Long Walk

• William Runs To The River

WILLIAM Wiseman stood in the center of Dunlap's Station and looked down at the Great Miami. The soldiers who could be spared a moment from their posts had drawn up to watch as he tried to get away.

Hundreds of Indians surrounded the stockade except on the river side. They would try to stop him from getting the letter in his pocket to General Harmar at Fort Washington. For if the General got the letter, he would send many soldiers against the Indians.

A soldier behind William called, "Remember, if you do make it over the river, you'll have to get back on this side before you can reach Fort Washington."

And someone else said, "When you have gone down the Great Miami about two miles, you'll find a place where you can wade across. Be careful. The water is swift and dangerous."

William Wiseman smiled. "I'll have to find that place. I can't swim," he said.

"Ready?" Lieutenant Kingsbury asked.

"Yes," William answered.

He crouched low and ran with his rifle in his hand down to the bank of the river. A man by the name of Krum and his 14-year-old son ran behind William. A boat lay hidden from the Indians behind a log on the shore. They helped William drag the boat to the edge of the river. William dropped his rifle into the bottom of the boat and sprang in, while they shoved it out into the water.

William had hardly left the bank when the Indians saw him. Bullets whizzed by his ears and above his head. He lost no time wondering how soon one of the bullets would strike him. He caught up a pole and sent the boat through the water.

He reached the opposite shore and sprang out. The Indians kept on shooting. Their bullets cut twigs and flakes of bark from the trees. He drew the canoe partly up the beach, and ran through the woods for a while. Then he came back towards the river. William wanted to stay near the Great Miami, but he had to be careful to keep out of sight of any Indians who might be following him on the opposite shore.

When William had run about two miles, he crawled through the underbrush to the edge of the river. There he sat and looked about the country. He saw no sign of Indians. He was safe!

• He Almost Drowns

Now he had to get back to the other side of the river. He searched for the place that was shallow enough to be waded. Not far from him the river was narrow. Although the water was fast, and full of mud and driftwood, he decided to cross at the narrow place in the river.

He stripped off his clothing. Holding his clothes, gun, bullet pouch, and powder horn well above his head, he walked into the water. He went on till the icy water came up to his chin, and the swift current almost knocked him off his feet. He wished he could swim. He knew that he would drown if he went even a step farther. If he drowned, General Harmar would never get the letter, and the settlers at Dunlap's Station would be killed by the Indians. He turned and came out of the river.

William walked along the river bank looking for the shallow place. He tried again when he had gone about a hundred yards. When he had waded almost halfway across, the water touched his chin. He turned back again. He was numb and blue with cold. He tried a third time. The water reached almost over his nose, and again he had to come back.

William now thought that he could never cross the river. He wondered if he should go to North Bend, but decided that this would not help. He thought of the people in the fort. They did not have enough food or water or bullets to hold out much longer against the Indians. He had to get soldiers to rescue the settlers of Dunlap's Station.

He determined to try to cross at another place along the river. When he had walked about a hundred yards farther, he thought he saw a chance to wade through the river to the other side. So for the fourth time he walked into the Great Miami. This time, when the water reached his waist, it came no higher. He went on. Soon he was across the river. Nothing but trees and hills, and maybe some of Girty's Indian scouts, now lay between him and Fort Washington.

He put his clothing on his shivering body. Then he started on his 15-mile journey through the forest, with no road or path to help him. He did not stop often to rest, for he had already lost time trying to get across the river. He stumbled on and on, until, at four o'clock in the afternoon, he saw through the trees the flag over Fort Washington.

William immediately delivered the letter to General Harmar. The General promised to help the people at Dunlap's Station, and praised William for his bravery. William listened to the praise and enjoyed it.

He liked even better something else the General said. William had fought for a day and a night. He had tried to wade the river three times, and had done it on the fourth time. Then he had run and walked many miles. During all these hardships, he had eaten only a little parched corn. So when General Harmar said, "My men will give you a good meal, and then you can go to bed," William was very glad indeed.

He Brings Help •

It would have been foolish to travel by night through country filled with Indians. The warriors might surprise and cut to pieces a good-sized army. So the soldiers waited impatiently for daylight.

As soon as the eastern sky brightened, William and other soldiers were up and away. They traveled on horseback, for they wanted to get to Dunlap's Station quickly.

They wondered if they would find the log walls and little cabins burned down and the men dead. If this were so, the Indians had probably carried away the women and children.

The soldiers need not have worried. They found Dunlap's Station and its people safe. There were no Indians around. When William Wiseman got away, Girty must have understood that sooner or later the young soldier would bring help. So Girty had ordered his Indians to leave.

The soldiers were sorry that they did not have the chance of beating Girty and his Indians. The people at Dunlap's Station were tired of fighting. They were glad that it was all over. But they did not soon forget William Wiseman. If the young soldier had not escaped the Indians, Girty would have continued the fighting until he destroyed the station and its people.

William Wiseman lived many years and had other adventures. But he never forgot the long walk he took to save Dunlap's Station. And when he was 80 years old, he wrote down the story.

• She told them to gather the nettles and bring them to her

7
Mother Finds a Way

• The River Upsets A Boat

EARLY on a spring morning in 1793 there was much excitement in the family of Alexander Guard. The children clapped their hands and danced around. Mrs. Guard herself was more quiet, but she, too, was happy.

They had lived for three years beside the Great Miami River near North Bend. Mr. Guard had just finished building a new log cabin farther down the river. Today they were moving.

A clumsy, home-made boat six or seven feet wide and more than 40 feet long was drawn up on the river bank below their home. Mr. and Mrs. Guard, together with the children large enough to help, were carrying all their furniture and household goods to the boat.

Mrs. Guard sometimes glanced at the Great Miami. She had a worried look in her eye. Spring rains had filled the river with swift water. She wished the big canoe were a flatboat. A big canoe, which was called a pirogue, could go quickly through the water, but it was not so safe as a flatboat. The sharp, narrow bottom of the pirogue made it easy to tip over. But there was no flatboat, nor could they carry their household goods down the river. So they had to use their canoe.

At last the boat was loaded with everything the Guard family had, and they were ready to start on their trip. Mrs. Guard and the children walked along the bank of the river. Mr. Guard got in the middle of the boat and paddled it downstream.

Mrs. Guard and the children could hardly keep up with Mr. Guard. The river was even more dangerous than they had thought. They watched Mr. Guard as he struggled to keep the boat straight in the water. Soon the current carried him to a bend in the river. The water swirled fast. The long boat was thrown around and overturned. Mr. Guard and all the family goods fell into the wild water.

Mrs. Guard and her children screamed, and ran toward him along the stream. They could see nothing except the pirogue whirling upside down in the muddy river.

After what seemed a long time, Mr. Guard's head bobbed up out of the water. Mr. Guard knew how to keep from being drowned. He did not struggle. He relaxed and swam until he reached his family on the shore. He stood there tired and dirty and dripping with water as they kissed him.

• Mrs. Guard Has A Problem

Mrs. Guard and the children were glad that he was alive and safe with them. They hardly gave a thought to their furniture and clothing lost in the river.

"We have one another, our new home, our land, and our farm animals," they said.

They walked on down the river to their new cabin. As they went, Mrs. Guard looked at her husband and children and wondered what she would do. They did not have enough money to buy new furniture. Even if they had, there was no furniture store in the wilderness. But Mr. Guard could make rough beds, tables, and three-legged stools from wood. He could gouge out bowls and whittle spoons, and could even make a spinning wheel and loom.

Mrs. Guard was not worried about furniture. She wondered how she would get clothes for her family. She had no cotton or wool or flax to spin. Her children could wear coonskin caps and deerskin moccasins. They might even sleep on skins, and use bear or buffalo robes for blankets. But Mr. Guard could not kill enough animals to get skins for the clothing of the whole family.

Mrs. Guard kept thinking about the problem of clothes for her family even after they had reached the new cabin. She kept worrying about it all through the days that she spent getting her house in order. She even wondered what to do about it as she planted corn, beans, pumpkins, and potatoes, and as she pulled weeds from the garden. She had a real problem to solve.

The children did not know that Mrs. Guard was worried. She smiled at them as they helped in the hard work of destroying the weeds. Some plants, such as pokeweeds, were easy to pluck, but others were tough to cut and hard to pull.

The toughest and hardest weeds to kill were the nettles. Their scratchy stems and prickly leaves stung the children's hands. All through the spring and summer Mrs. Guard pulled nettles and kept worrying about winter clothing for her children. One day she found some nettles that seemed especially tough. She stopped her work in the garden and looked at them carefully. She saw there were strong fibers in the stem. She pulled the fibers apart. Then she stood a long time trying to work out something in her mind.

The next morning her children were surprised when she told them to gather the nettles and bring them to her. "I want all I can get," she said.

The boys and girls found many nettles all around. They cut the rough plants and brought them to their mother. They wondered what she would do with them, and watched her as she began to work out her idea with the plants.

She Solves It •

Mrs. Guard cut away the leaves and pounded the stems until the pulp was loosened. Then she soaked the bruised stems in water. She left them in the water for several days. When she took them out, the bark and softer parts of the stems were ready to fall away. Mrs. Guard then dried and combed the stems with a wire brush until nothing was left but the strong fibers. Then she spread out the fibers on the grass to bleach.

Next Mrs. Guard began spinning the fibers into thread as she would have spun flax for linen. Soon she had a good deal of thread. It was coarse and yellowish brown, but strong enough to be woven into cloth.

Mr. Guard built a loom, and Mrs. Guard began weaving. The work went slowly. She liked the cloth she wove, and asked the children to gather more nettles. They ran out eagerly, and came back with their arms full of nettles. Their mother wove more cloth. When she thought she had enough cloth, Mrs. Guard made it up into dresses and coats and trousers.

When winter came, the children put on heavy clothes. And as they played in them and were warm, they were thankful that they had such a wise mother.

• "Mad" Anthony's men staged make-believe battles

8
Big Wind

• Bad News Comes From The North

THE log fire blazed and crackled on the hearth. Outside, the November wind moaned through the great trees on the hills behind the little town of Cincinnati. Eight-year-old William Ludlow shivered, and came near the fire. His six-year-old sister, Elizabeth, sat on the floor with her knees drawn up and her arms around her legs. She looked into the fire with frightened eyes as she listened to grownups telling fearsome tales of the Indians. Both children were too excited to eat the chestnuts they had just roasted.

The Indians were troublesome. They stole horses and cattle, captured women and children, and killed hunters and travelers. The United States Government had tried to make peace with them. When the Indians refused to promise not to bother the white men, General Harmar had been sent against them with an army of soldiers. He had been defeated. Next General St. Clair had come and marched away with many men. At Cincinnati and in the stations among the hills to the north, the settlers waited for news of St. Clair's army.

Tonight word had come through frightened messengers. The Indians had surprised the army of St. Clair and killed and wounded great numbers of his men.

William listened to the talk and looked at his father and mother and the other grown people. He knew they were afraid. He could see the fear in their eyes. They were sure the Indians would make more and fiercer raids on the settlements.

The settlers were sad that winter. Many people moved away as the Indians grew bolder. Every night, as the family sat about the fire, William heard tales of the dark deeds of the Indians. They slipped from the hills and stole from the settlers who lived where Sycamore, Main, and Broadway Streets go down on the river bank. Each man carried his rifle with him wherever he went. If he forgot to take his gun to church, he was arrested and had to pay some money.

William was never allowed to stray into the woods, but he did go to school. The schoolhouse was a log building near the foot of Main Street. It was close to the river and Fort Washington. At school the boys talked of the Indian trouble and wondered what general would next try to conquer the Indians. Harmar had failed and St. Clair had failed. The settlers and the Indians were beginning to think that no one could succeed.

• Good News Comes From The East

The autumn of 1792 came, and the hopes of the settlers rose. They heard that the Government was sending another general and another army against the Indians.

The general was Anthony Wayne. Few of the settlers had ever seen General Wayne, but many had heard of him. He had fought through the Revolutionary War and was known as a man who was never afraid. Some had nicknamed him "Mad" Anthony Wayne.

"Mad" Anthony Wayne was cautious now. He did not go to Cincinnati immediately. He drilled his men all through the winter, then came down the river with them as the April rain was raising the river almost to the doorsteps of the cabins in Cincinnati.

The only suitable dry place for a camp in Cincinnati was the ground where Fifth Street now crosses Mound Street. This area came to be known as Camp Hobson's Choice. When you do something whether or not you want to, it is called a Hobson's Choice. You actually have no choice, just as Wayne had no choice.

The soldiers drilled and practiced all summer long.

Four hundred men soon came up from Kentucky to join Wayne's army. They were not dressed in the uniforms of soldiers. They looked like hunters. Powder horns were slung over their shoulders. Their guns were as long as a tall man. They wore deerskin hunting shirts down almost to their knees. On their heads were coonskin caps, and their feet were in moccasins. Although they did not look or dress like the other soldiers, they knew how to fight Indians. They were the kind of men General Wayne wanted in his army, and he welcomed them.

The village was filled with noise. Always there was the talk about Indians and about "Mad" Anthony Wayne's chances of defeating them.

William listened to the talk. He got used to it and to seeing soldiers in the town. He liked the sound of muskets, the tramp of feet, and the roll of drums.

Sundays were especially exciting. They were the days on which "Mad" Anthony's men staged make-believe battles. General Wayne stood on the top of a high mound. He watched the soldiers and called his orders. No matter how much noise there might be, the men heard him.

William would climb a nearby beech tree and sit on one of its limbs. He watched and heard all that went on. General Wayne commanded an officer to take a company of riflemen in among the trees. The riflemen would whoop and yell, making war cries as if they were Indians. The other soldiers would fight the make-believe Indians. There were, of course, no bullets in their muskets.

William wondered what all this was for. Wayne's men were supposed to march against the Indians. Why did they waste so much time playing "Soldier and Indians"?

Big Wind Sweeps Through The North •

One day General Wayne and his army marched out of town. They went up Main Street, then turned northwest up the Mill Creek Valley toward the Indian towns. As the soldiers passed, men, women, and children waved goodbye. The people feared they would never see the soldiers again.

The settlers went home to their cabins and waited for news. Now and then they heard of the doings of General Wayne. He had sent scouts to search the country for Indians. He did not want the Indians to take him by surprise, as they had done to General St. Clair.

The Indian tribes knew General Wayne was coming. They called him Big Wind because of the swift, forceful way he came into their country with many men.

The Indian chiefs held a council of war. Some were not certain they should try to fight "Mad" Anthony. Little Turtle, one of the greatest of the chiefs, shook his head. "He is a general who never sleeps. The night and day are to him alike. We cannot win," he said. But the other chiefs wished to fight. "We conquered Harmar. We conquered St. Clair. We shall conquer Big Wind," they said.

Meanwhile, William's father had moved from Cincinnati to White's Station, which was a small, lonely place on Mill Creek where Carthage now stands. Here William heard how General Wayne was fighting the Indians. He was beginning to understand why Wayne had spent so much time drilling in Cincinnati. He wondered whether "Mad" Anthony would win.

One day William was sleeping under a tree which kept the August sun from his face. He awoke suddenly. His father was shouting, "William, William, wake up! 'Mad' Anthony has beaten the Indians!"

William listened to the story of Wayne's battle with the Indians, which had taken place on the Maumee River near the present city of Toledo. "Mad" Anthony's men had fought from behind fallen logs in a forest, and the battle was therefore called the Battle of Fallen Timbers.

William was glad that the Indians would no longer trouble his family and his neighbors. He and his father would not be afraid to work in their fields, and he could go to the woods to hunt the cows or gather pawpaws. Big Wind had swept away the danger.

• He went forth

9
Doctor Goforth and the Collapsible Lion

• The Doctor Is A Dandy

WHEN Cincinnati was a little village, its people had to work hard in the fields and in the woods. So they wore the rough clothes of farmers and hunters. That is, all did except one. This strange man always wore fancy clothes, with ruffles and buckles and bright gold buttons.

Whenever this gentleman went out, he put a wig over his own hair and sprinkled powder on it. Then he pulled a pair of neat gloves on his hands and tucked a gold-headed cane under his arm. Dressed in this way, the man would step his shiny-buckled shoes onto the dusty street. People would stare at him as he strode down the street or got up on his horse or knocked at the door of somebody's cabin.

The man's name was Doctor William Goforth. He went forth at all hours even in bad weather to care for sick people. Sometimes the Doctor would get out of bed quickly in the middle of the night, put on his fine clothes, and ride on his horse eight or ten miles to treat someone taken sick in a hurry.

Doctor Goforth would go to all who sent for him. It did not matter much whether they were rich or poor. His pay for a short visit was a few cents, and feed for his horse. If a patient was very poor, the Doctor charged even less. For sitting up all night with a sick person, he never asked more than a dollar.

Since there were few doctors in this backwoods country, Doctor Goforth had patients as far away as Ludlow's Station and Milford. He also served the people across the Ohio River in Kentucky. When he had to visit them, he could not ride his horse, for there was as yet no bridge over the river. So he took up his small leather bag and crossed the Ohio on a ferryboat. Then he clambered up the river bank and set out on foot to the homes of his patients.

The Doctor was welcomed wherever he went. The children looked at his powdered wig and touched his shiny cane. The women were pleased by his polite ways. The men laughed at his jokes.

Everybody liked to hear him talk. He would sit a long time and tell funny stories which he said were true. When he recited these tales, his eyes twinkled and the words went out of his mouth slowly. But when one of his listeners started to talk about gold or old bones, Doctor Goforth's eyes got excited and he talked fast.

He would say, "There's gold in those hills around Cincinnati."
The people listening would then ask, "How do you know, Doctor?"

• Old Bones Lead Him Astray

This question made Doctor Goforth move back in his chair and talk a long while. He told them that he paid men to go into the hills and look around for gold. He was sure that they would find it any day.

The people knew why he wanted to find gold, which could buy the Doctor many things. But they did not know why he wanted bones.

"How about those old bones you're looking for, Doctor Goforth?" they would ask. "Are you finding any? Suppose you do, of what good are they? Even dogs won't eat them. They're as hard as stone."

Doctor Goforth would smile fondly at them and explain why he was so anxious to know when they happened to come across a big old bone in the fields or beside the creeks. He told them that many, many years ago, huge animals lived here. After the great beasts died, he said, their bones turned to stone from lying around so long in the soil. Nobody in Doctor Goforth's time knew what these animals had looked like. So the Doctor and a few other men wanted to put together the old bones they found and see whether they could get some idea of what the animals looked like when they were alive.

After Doctor Goforth had said all this, it was usually time for him to go. But he was still explaining to them as he got together his things and went slowly out to his horse.

As he rode away, he would call back, "Just wait and see. Some day I'll be able to piece together the skeleton of a strange animal."

The people would stand around watching him go. Then they shook their heads. They liked Doctor Goforth. They could not believe that what he told about bones was true, but they said, "Anyway, he's a good doctor. And he's dependable. He comes whenever we need him."

One day in the spring of 1802, the Doctor's patients sent for him, but he did not come. They were surprised, and wondered if he were sick. Several men went to Cincinnati and knocked on the door of Doctor Goforth's house. There was no answer. They walked down the street and met a woman about to enter her cabin to get dinner.

"We are looking for Doctor Goforth," they said. "Perhaps you know where we can find him?"

The woman laughed as she unfastened her bonnet and pushed open the door of her house.

"I can, in a way. He's down the river somewhere," she said. "He told everybody that he was going to look for old bones."

The men opened their eyes wide, and put their fingers on their beards. They were sorry for the doctor, for they thought he had lost his mind. The men returned to their families and told them what had happened. They all mourned Doctor Goforth as if he were dead.

"He was such a good doctor," the women said, as they put their handkerchiefs to their faces.

He Brings Them Back •

Nothing was heard of Doctor Goforth for a while. Suddenly he appeared again. His fine clothes were not so neat as usual, and his horse looked tired. But the Doctor himself was red in the face and happy. With him were several men on horses holding up big bags full of something heavy. The Doctor stored the bags in his house, paid the men, and went to bed.

The next day Doctor Goforth started to visit his patients. As he came to each cabin, he shouted greetings. The people ran out of the house. They were overjoyed to see their good doctor looking healthy. They welcomed him into the house, and asked him many questions. They wanted to know where he had been, what he had done, what he had found, and how he felt.

Doctor Goforth smiled as if he would soon tell them in his own way what they were so anxious to know.

"Now, wait a moment, please," he said. "I'll tell you everything in good time."

He made the settlers more curious by keeping quiet and looking as if he were about to talk. Then he began his story.

"Not long ago I learned from some Indians that they had seen many old bones at a place on the Kentucky side of the Ohio River. The place is called Big Bone Lick. For several days I thought about what they told me. Then I decided that these were the kind of old bones I was looking for."

"How did you know they were, Doctor?" one of the men asked.

"Well," Doctor Goforth replied, "I knew that the Indians and settlers lead their horses and cows to Big Bone Lick because there is much salt in the clay soil there. I thought that, many years ago, the huge animals I told you about may also have gone to Big Bone Lick to get salt."

"But why would their bones be there? Did they die eating salt?" asked the mother of the family listening.

"No," smiled Doctor Goforth, "but the animals must have fought to get near the salt. They did not simply peck at each other the way chickens do when you feed them. The big animals bit and clawed until one of them was dead. Then the other licked the salt and went away, leaving the dead animal where it had fallen."

One of the eager little boys who was listening said, "Doctor Goforth, maybe it happened this way. Perhaps an animal was licking salt. Then a bigger animal came up and ate the smaller one, leaving only the bones."

"Yes," said Doctor Goforth, "that also may have happened. Anyway, I hired several men and went to Big Bone Lick to see whether I was right. I was. We dug up many huge bones."

• They Go Abroad

The children jumped up excitedly, clapped their hands, and cried, "Where are they?"

"I brought them back with me. They are now in my cabin," said the Doctor.

"What are you going to do with them?" asked the mother.

"I'm going to fit them together and see what those big animals used to be like," replied the Doctor, as he got up to leave.

"May we help? Please, Doctor Goforth, may we help you?" begged the children, as they danced around and pulled at his sleeve all the way to his horse.

"Yes, you may," said the Doctor, getting up on the horse, "whenever your parents bring you to my house in Cincinnati."

After Doctor Goforth had talked to each family about his trip, he went back to Cincinnati, and started to fit the many bones together. Sometimes children and their parents would come to watch him and to help. It was a hard, slow job, like piecing together a big newspaper that has been torn into hundreds of pieces, with some of the pieces missing.

During the next few years, Doctor Goforth in his spare time tried to fit the bones together. One evening, while he was working very hard and wondering if he would ever get them into their right places, he heard a knock at the door.

"Come in," said the Doctor, without even glancing up. He was used to people coming to look at the bones.

The door opened, and a gentleman as finely dressed as Doctor Goforth himself stepped into the room. He introduced himself as Thomas E. Ashe, and said he had just come from London, England. He told Doctor Goforth that finding the bones had made the Doctor a great man. He said that learned men in London had sent him to tell the Doctor that they would like to borrow the bones and try to fit them together.

Doctor Goforth was pleased that news of his finding the bones had traveled all the way across the Atlantic Ocean. He told Mr. Ashe that he would gladly loan him the bones to take to the learned men in London.

Mr. Ashe thanked Doctor Goforth and left. Next day he sent men around to the Doctor's house to put the bones in bags and load the bags on a stagecoach. Then Mr. Ashe got into the coach and was driven away.

Doctor Goforth waited anxiously to learn what had become of the bones. In those days, it took many months to bring newspapers across the ocean to this country, then over the mountains and down the Ohio River to Cincinnati. After a long time, Doctor Goforth received a London newspaper which told about the bones he had dug up.

They Do Strange Things •

A column in the paper said that Mr. Ashe had put together several huge skeletons, the bones of which he had found in America. Mr. Ashe told the English people that one of the skeletons once belonged to a lion 60 feet long and 25 feet high. He also said that the lion had ribs which folded up like an accordion when the lion crouched. When the animal wanted to jump, the ribs opened and sent him into the air like a jack-in-the-box. Mr. Ashe claimed that such collapsible lions still lived in America beyond the Mississippi River.

Doctor Goforth was not pleased when he read about Mr. Ashe taking credit for finding the bones. But he was glad to read about the bones belonging to such a wonderful animal as a collapsible lion. He hurried around to all his patients, and showed them the newspaper. He talked for hours about his collapsible lion, and said that he would soon get the bones back so that his patients could see the skeleton of the remarkable animal.

Doctor Goforth never did get his bones back, and he died thinking that he had found a collapsible lion. We now know there never was such a creature as a collapsible lion. What Doctor Goforth actually discovered were the bones of a huge sloth having three toes. It was an ancestor of the three-toed sloths that now hang from trees in South America and in the zoo. Doctor Goforth's sloth never did hang from a tree because there was no tree large enough for it to hang from. It was truly a strange animal, but not quite so strange as a collapsible lion.

• She cackled and called and scolded

10
The Playmates

• Edward Gets A Gift

CUMMINSVILLE has not always been called Cumminsville. Once it was known as Ludlow's Station, in honor of the man who built the first log cabin in Losantiville. It was then a group of cabins within a small stockade. Nothing but hills and trees stood between the stockade and Cincinnati.

Then in 1796 Colonel Israel Ludlow came with his beautiful bride, and built for her a fine home. For several years Mrs. Ludlow was very happy here with her children. Then one cold day in January, 1804, Colonel Ludlow died. The next year a family named Mansfield moved into the neighborhood.

Mrs. Ludlow had a little girl named Sara Bella. The child had pretty yellow hair and blue eyes. The Mansfields had a little boy about her age, named Edward. He had bright eyes and curly hair. Sara Bella and Edward liked to play together.

One day the little boy was sorry to hear that Sara Bella was leaving. Her family was moving back to Cincinnati, five miles away.

The day her family moved, Sara Bella came hunting young Edward. She had a small wooden tub in her arms. "I've brought you something," she said.

Edward wondered what it could be. He looked into the tub and saw many eggs. The eggs were larger than hens' eggs, and were bluish-white instead of pure white or brown.

Edward laughed. "I could never eat so many duck eggs," he said.

Sara Bella laughed, too. "You're not supposed to *eat* them," she said. "Put them under a setting hen. Then wait and see what happens."

Edward went to the barn and found a clucking hen sitting on a nest. She pecked at him and ruffled her feathers when he went near. He was not afraid. He slipped the eggs under her. The hen settled on the eggs and began to cluck softly.

Every day Edward came to the barn to see if the hen was still on the eggs. Soon he saw that he did not have to worry. The hen kept the eggs warm day and night. She left the nest only when she wanted to eat. If the day was cold, she stayed away only a little while and then came running back to her nest before the eggs would get cold.

Edward counted the days. When 21 days had gone, he peeped into the nest. He knew that chickens come 21 days after the eggs are put under the hen.

It Changes Into Ducks

When Edward saw no signs of anything breaking through the shells, he went to the house and told his mother that the eggs were not hatching as they should.

His mother laughed and said, "You are hatching ducks, not chickens. It takes a duck egg a week longer to hatch than a chicken egg."

Edward waited seven more days and went to the nest again. He wanted to peep under to see if his ducks had come out of the eggs. The hen pecked at him so fiercely that he could not get his hand into the nest. He stood a few feet away and listened. When the hen stopped her loud clucking, he heard soft little noises. He knew the eggs were hatching, and he ran to tell his mother.

"You must not bother the hen," his mother said, "but maybe we had better see if the eggs are getting along all right."

Mrs. Mansfield lifted the hen gently so as not to hurt the hatching eggs. Edward stood by his mother and peeped in. Two tiny feathered things had broken through their eggshells and were huddled in the nest. They had webbed feet and were as brightly yellow as dandelions. Another little duck was halfway out. While Edward watched, he saw the bill of a fourth duckling come pecking through its shell.

"Now leave them alone. Don't go bothering them. The old hen knows more about such things than you," Mrs. Mansfield told Edward as she put the hen back on the nest.

All through that day Edward kept going to the nest. But he obeyed his mother. He did not bother the hen. Soon he saw the yellow heads of two ducks peeping out from under the hen's feathers. They were eager to see where they were.

After a while Mrs. Mansfield came out to look. She saw that all of the eggs had hatched. In the nest were 17 fluffy yellow ducklings, peeping and squirming and stretching up their little necks. They opened wide their little flat bills, as if saying, "We're hungry." Mrs. Mansfield picked up the mother hen and set her aside. Then she put the little ducks in her apron and carried them out to the barnyard.

Edward ran to the kitchen. He brought out a piece of cornbread and crumbled it on the ground near his new pets. Then he stood by and watched the mother hen. She took a crumb of bread in her bill, but did not eat it. She spread her wings and made low noises. She seemed to be telling the baby ducks that bread was good to eat. She nodded her head and explained how they should pick up the crumbs. The little ducks understood, and they began to eat.

Edward laughed at the way they ate. The hen picked at the food with her sharp bill. The little ducks did not have sharp bills. Theirs were flat on the top and bottom and round at the end. So they used their bills like shovels and scooped up the crumbs.

The Ducks Make Mischief •

Although "Mad" Anthony Wayne had made the country safe for white men, it was still not safe for ducks. Hungry foxes and weasels prowled in the hills about Cumminsville. At night wolves howled and wildcats screamed. They would eat the ducks if they got the chance.

Edward took good care of his ducks. Every night he went to see that they were safely huddled under the hen in the barn. Each morning he counted them to see whether any was missing. He watered and fed them, and he did not let them wander into the woods.

When he was not looking, the ducks were in danger. Hawks flew over the barnyard. They liked to grab small ducks and fly away with them. But the stepmother of the ducks was a smart old hen. She watched for the hawks. When she saw one, she would cackle loudly. The young ducks would run to her, and she would whisper to them to huddle under her and be quiet. They kept so still that the hawk flying overhead never knew anything was in the barnyard except a big hen with great wings stretched out.

Whenever Edward heard the hen making a noise as if she saw a hawk, he always came running to frighten the hawk away. One day he heard the old hen making a terrible fuss. She cackled and called and scolded. It sounded as if she were greatly excited by some new trouble that had happened to her duck children.

Edward thought a hawk or a snake was killing the ducks. He dashed out to find the hen. She was not in the barnyard. He hunted all around, and found her nearby on the bank of Mill Creek. She was fussing back and forth at the edge of the water, with her feathers straight up and her wings flapping. She cackled and called and scolded.

Edward looked at her. Then he looked at the creek. He laughed and laughed. He called his brothers and sisters. They all looked and laughed. They felt a little sorry for the troubled old hen. She could not swim, so she supposed that her stepchildren could not either. She was afraid they would drown.

Although the old hen cackled and scolded, the little ducks paid no attention to her and kept paddling up and down the creek. When the old hen could not call them out, and she saw they did not drown, she began to look disgusted instead of frightened.

As the ducks grew older, they spent more and more of their time on the creek. The yellow down that covered them fell away, and white feathers came in its place. Edward looked and looked, but he could not find a single black feather. The ducks were pure white.

Soon they were big enough to get along without help from the old hen. Their wings grew wide and strong. They could fly up from the creek into the trees or over the barnyard fence.

• They Take A Trip

There were many wild ducks about Ludlow's Station. Sometimes they would come flying overhead and settle down on the water beside the tame ducks. The tame ducks looked at them and listened to their call and quacking. Edward wondered what the wild ducks were saying to his tame ducks.

The autumn came, and the air grew chilly. The wild birds started south for the winter. Edward heard wild geese call, "Honk, honk," as they flew far above the treetops. He also heard the hoarse cry of the wild ducks. He watched all these wild birds flying so high that his eyes watered and hurt to see them become black dots against the sky.

One day, while Edward's ducks were having fun in the creek, the wild ducks came again. They quacked loudly to the white tame ducks. Maybe they told the tame ducks where they were going. Perhaps they said it was a place where a duck could swim all winter because there was no ice on the water. Maybe they talked of blue water in the Gulf of Mexico, or of dark swamps in Florida, or of wild rice along the Mississippi River.

Whatever it was the wild ducks said, the white ducks listened. Edward saw his ducks suddenly take to the sky and go flying south with their wild cousins. He thought his ducks were not thankful for all he had done for them. He was *so* sad. He would miss playing with them.

One day, as Edward stood beside the creek wondering what his ducks were doing, he heard a great flapping of wings. Seventeen pure white ducks came flying down to the water beside him. They were his tame ducks. They had come home to the place they loved and the playmate who loved them.

THE END